Building Your Child's Self-Esteem

Also by Yvonne Brooks

100 Ways to Become a Successful Teenager

Kids Success Journal

Intellectual Parenting Skills

Intellectual Parenting Skills Journal

Kids Finance 101

Financial Planning for Teens

Financial Warfare

Daily Financial Journal

Financial Confessions

Proverbs 101 for Kids

Building Your Child's Self-Esteem

9 Secrets Every Parent Needs to Know

Yvonne Brooks

iUniverse, Inc.
Bloomington

Building Your Child's Self-Esteem
9 Secrets Every Parent Needs to Know

iUniverse books may be ordered through booksellers or by contacting:

iUniverse
1663 Liberty Drive
Bloomington, IN 47403
www.iuniverse.com
1-800-Authors (1-800-288-4677)

Because of the dynamic nature of the Internet, any web addresses or links contained in this book may have changed since publication and may no longer be valid. The views expressed in this work are solely those of the author and do not necessarily reflect the views of the publisher, and the publisher hereby disclaims any responsibility for them.

Any people depicted in stock imagery provided by Thinkstock are models, and such images are being used for illustrative purposes only.

Certain stock imagery © Thinkstock.

ISBN: 978-1-4697-4675-3 (sc)
ISBN: 978-1-4697-4677-7 (hc)
ISBN: 978-1-4697-4676-0 (e)

Printed in the United States of America

iUniverse rev. date: 01/26/2012

Self-esteem is your sense of personal worth. It encompasses both self-confidence and self-acceptance.

In part, healthy self-esteem comes from your awareness of the value you add to your family and the community.

Table of Contents

Introduction

Welcome to all parents, guardians, teachers, and anyone interested in improving the self-esteem of children! While primarily directed toward parents, _Building Your Child's Self-Esteem_ can serve as, a resource for all adults who want to positively influence the lives of children. This book's goal is to strategically add value and fun to children's daily lives, and to the lives of the adults responsible for them.

Those working with children will experience many benefits when applying the information contained in this book. Nothing is more essential to a happy and successful childhood than healthy self-esteem!

Children with healthy self-esteem:

- Show greater respect and honor in the home
- Have an enhanced ability to learn
- Think proactively, are more independent, and are more successful in self-management
- Enjoy mutually beneficial relationships with their parents and others
- Discover unlimited opportunities to add value not only to their families, but also to their communities

Self-esteem is transferable! Children with healthy self-esteem tend to come from environments where parents, guardians, and teachers also demonstrate healthy self-esteem. Similarly, children with low self-esteem are often the product of environments where parents, guardians, and other adults demonstrate disorder, disrespect, poor discipline, irresponsibility, lack of self-growth and poor communication skills.

You can add value to a child's life by understanding how to cultivate an atmosphere conducive to creating and maintaining a healthy self-esteem.

Consider this startling question: What if "behavior problems", did not exist, and the children exhibiting them were merely manifesting "low self-esteem"?

An understanding of this revolutionary concept can lead to long-term changes that _empower_ children. Children with healthy self-esteem add value not only to themselves, but also to others, in their own families, in schools and communities. The reach of that ripple effect is infinite.

You now hold in your hands a step-by-step guide, with clear and concise instructions, for improving the level of any child's self-esteem. In the right environment, children can learn to "self-correct"– eradicate negative behaviors by means of their own independent and responsible behavior, and mind-set.

This book will give you nine secrets-_plus bonus materials!_ -that will help you cultivate healthy, confident, and courageous children effortlessly!

How Self-Esteem Manifests in Children

Manifestations of Healthy Self-Esteem
Children with healthy self-esteem choose to manage their own potential so they can succeed by:
- Overcoming negative thoughts
- Learning how to modify behaviors that need improvement
- Practicing self-control
- Having good vocabulary
- Communicating effectively

This book will show you how to coach children in fulfilling their destinies and achieving their goals.

Behaviors of Children with Healthy Self-esteem:
Children with healthy self-esteem are visionaries who:
- Take personal responsibility for their own behavior
- Focus on priorities
- Limit distractions that reduce growth and productivity

Research by The Johnson O'Connor Research Foundation (www .jcrf.org/) has shown an incredibly strong correlation between the following: the importance of communication in early child development, children's vocabulary skills, their self-esteem and their potential for success in life. Help your children by paying particular attention to your children's communication skills.

Sayings of Children with Healthy Self-esteem:

"I am persistent"
    Many children with healthy self-esteem use this powerful saying
    to move themselves forward.

"All I need is within me"
    Victorious children will frequently say this for reasons including:

    1. They have entered a higher level of understanding, which
        ignites a confidence in knowing, that most problems have
        multiple solutions.
    2. They believe in their own innate ability to discover and
        implement this understanding.

Manifestations of Low Self-Esteem
Children with low self-esteem:
*   Easily become victims of deception, manipulation, and
    even abuse
*   React to people and events automatically based on
    "appearance"
*   Usually entertain a selfish-dominated mentality
*   Easily become bullies who deceive, manipulate, and/or
    victimize others

Most victims have very low self-esteem, which attracts bullies
to them. (Ironically bullies also have very low self-esteem).
Bullies find other children, both victims and other bullies, who
mirror their own negative and destructive thought patterns of
"worthlessness".

The interdependence of victims and bullies perpetuates the cycle
of deception, manipulation, and victimization.

Behaviors of Children with Low Self-Esteem:
Children with low self-esteem:
- Constantly complain
- Exhibit thoughts that reveal their high level of self-hatred (their self-talk, body language, and conversations with others often exhibit this as well)
- Blame others
- Refuse self-responsibility

Blaming others is a clear sign of low self-esteem and victimization. Children who are unclear about the value they add to their families and their communities often cast blame; this tendency, if uncorrected, will continue into adolescence and adulthood.

Sayings of Children with Low Self-Esteem:

"I can't do it."
Children who see themselves as "victims" rather than "achievers" will often say this in response to anything that frightens or challenges them.

"It's too hard."
This is a typical response from children who reject knowledge and refuse to rise to excellence.

Parent/Child Activities
You will soon notice that there are two types of activities placed strategically throughout this book: activities for parents to undertake personally, and activities for parents to use with their children.

You might wonder, "Why include activities for parents to personally perform, and questions for parents to personally answer?" (Thanks for asking that logical question! You did ask, right?) Here's the straightforward answer: Parents' own level of self-esteem is one of the most powerful influencers of children's self-esteem, especially in early childhood.

As you read further, you will encounter numerous exercises designed to give children opportunities to think about and contribute to the welfare of their own families, schools, and surrounding communities. Children with low self-esteem often fail to see, avail themselves of, or even care about such opportunities. Practice allows children to develop competence, which in turn, breeds confidence.

As children grow they need to learn effective self-management in order to deal with an increased degree/amount of trials, tribulations, hardships, and they do need to learn how to do this without complaining. By encouraging children to practice competence-building tasks in early childhood, parents and other influential adults can play a major role in developing, maintaining, and increasing a child's self-esteem. Using the opportunity to improve a child's life by teaching them how to improve their own healthy self-esteem starts with you!

(AUTHOR'S NOTE: The exercises in this book are not age specific. Some will be more useful with younger children; others with older children. Use the exercises most appropriate for your children, and feel free to modify them, and/or create your own versions.)

How to Maximize the Value of This Book:

By following the six steps outlined below you can maximize this book's value-for you and your children. (If you are not a parent, please substitute your role-guardian, teacher, etc-when reading the text below and throughout this book.)

Step 1:

Before you begin, write down your purpose for reading this book. (a written purpose helps focus the brain, allowing it, to recognize and decode the upcoming secrets you need to best help your child).

Step 2:

Take some time to consider and answer the following questions:

1. What will it take for me to raise my personal self-esteem? (I know that by doing so, I will add value not only to myself, but also to my children.)
2. What stimulates my desire for excellence?
3. What are my personal visions for improving my own health, my knowledge, my finances, my family relationships, and my community?
4. Who are my role models for building strong and healthy self-esteem?
5. What resources will I need to strengthen myself as a parent to cultivate healthy self-esteem?

As you become more self-aware, you will increase your ability to connect the new information you are about to learn with what you already know about building healthy self-esteem.

Step 3:

Write down what you want to know about and learn from each of the nine secrets.

- Preview the information written in this book (review the table of contents, skim the headings, etc), and formulate questions for each section.
- Imagine in advance how each secret will help you add value to yourself and your children.

Step 4:

Allow plenty of time to absorb new ideas:

- Create a schedule for reading, (fifteen to thirty minute increments should work well). There's no hurry to finish this book.
- Always read with a dictionary alongside, and take time to look up the definitions of any unfamiliar words (the better you understand the terminology, the more you will comprehend and be able to apply that knowledge to your children's situations and goals, as well as your own).

Step 5:

Make plans and take action!

- At the end of each reading session, write down at least one idea for how to use what you've learned with your children.
- Implement every new idea within twenty-four hours, (it is vital to move from knowledge to action, because without it, knowledge is useless).

Step 6:

Learn to use affirmations and quotes (look for these at the end of each chapter, also see Appendix A for a longer list). These are short, powerful, and positive statements that promote healthy self-esteem and immediately have a powerful impact on us. Our thoughts help create our reality, in turn helping us, and our children to move toward our desired futures.

Both you and your children should think, say and memorize the affirmations and quotes daily. You will be amazed at their transformative power.

In addition, be sure to read the story at the beginning of each section. They illustrate the power of each secret, reflect composite characters, (not actual children), and the positive outcomes are real, and _absolutely_ attainable.

This book contains another essential section called "Bonus Secret: The Power of Real Connection." Designed to work in tandem with the nine secrets, this section addresses the ongoing issue of the parent/child relationship in our hypermediated, cyber-oriented world. Social media (Facebook, Twitter, texting, computer games, TV, and so on), all can foster isolation-and even bullying –despite their purporting to increase "social connection." The only effective, lasting solution for those various interactions is true connection with actual "live" experiences between parents, their children, and among family members. This bonus section offers advice and tips on how to help you establish real, lasting connections, and help your children practice and enjoy healthy self-esteem in both the real and virtual worlds.

Lastly, you will notice a section called "Scriptural Secrets". That abounds with wisdom on parenting and healthy self-esteem; If the secrets in this section resonate with you, please use them, but If not, feel free to find wise thoughts that do elsewhere in this book. The combination of each tool contained in this book is essential for building healthy self-esteem.

Secrets are things known only to oneself or to a few others. This book contains nine such secrets.

Are you ready for the secrets to be revealed?

Let's begin!

Secret # 1:
The Power of Love

Story About Love

At age eight, Clayton had sustained a serious injury, when a rottweiler bit him two centimeters from his eye. Patiently and lovingly, his dad told him he was the same boy that he had been before the accident. They continued to do all the family things they had done before, and Clayton's parents found safe ways for him to engage in activities as he progressed through the healing process.

After long months of recuperation and therapy, Clayton was back playing with the same dog, but a physical and emotional scar remained. Teasing persisted in school –so much, that he begged to stay home, even though he was a straight A-student who loved to learn. Clayton's parents continued to focus on his accomplishments, praising his consistently excellent grades. They told him "the accident was something that had happened, he couldn't change that fact, but that he didn't have to allow the accident to define who he was".

Joshua, (a fellow fifth-grader who teased Clayton the most about his scar), was a fifth-grader just like Clayton, but unlike Clayton, he was very athletic, but not a terribly good student. In class, Clayton made it a point to never snicker or make jokes when Joshua would answer a question incorrectly or be the last one to turn in his test paper. After a while, Joshua seemed to notice, and one day, offered to walk Clayton to the school bus after school.

As the school bus began to load, Joshua and Clayton waved good-bye to each other. Later, Clayton relayed to his parents, his interaction with Joshua at school earlier in the day.

"I don't know why he walked me to the school bus today, I thought he hated me."

His dad responded, "I think he noticed your kindness in the classroom, so he wanted to be kind to you. That's a very good thing." Said Clayton's dad.

Clayton agreed, and knowing that Joshua did not have a mom and dad who helped him the way his parents did, he wanted to do even more to help Joshua.

The next day when they got to school, Clayton went up to Joshua. "I sure wish I could run as fast as you", he said.

Joshua grinned. "Whenever you're ready, I would love to go running with you."

"I'd like that!" Clayton smiled back. "I am really only good at school stuff."

"I wish I could read faster." Joshua said with enthusiasm.

"I can help you with that." Clayton said with excitement.

And so Clayton started helping Joshua with his homework, and Joshua started helping Clayton learn the physical techniques for running in a safe and fun way. Joshua's grades were never as good as Clayton's and Clayton never won a race. However, they taught each other the meaning of "unconditional love", that what matters is loving yourself as you are, because that is what will allow you to love others as they are. When we practice the power of love daily, we heal ourselves naturally, and transformation of our families and our communities becomes effortless.

Defining the Power of Love:
Love is the first trait of healthy self-esteem. Like self-esteem, love is highly transferable from adults to children.

Love is a "noun", and it is also a "verb". As such, it has to be acted upon in order to be credible. Love is a motivator that causes us to respond to others with our "actions", not just our "words".

Every child requires love to survive. At an early age, children should be taught at an early age the tools for attending to their own needs of love before they can become responsible for loving others with authenticity.

Do you have negative thoughts about how others perceive you? Displaying love is the easiest way to disarm those thoughts. You were magnificently and wonderfully created for a purpose. The time of that purpose is now! Our world needs you. Your love is the answer to improving your family and community relationships.

As adults we know what the negative impact of a lack of love has in our lives. Imagine how much more of a deeper negative impact that has on a child. Without loving parents (or a loving guardian), many children experience frustration and loneliness. However; because love is powerful and transformative, this can be changed! As you personally practice sincere love, your inner strength will increase and you will build your own self-esteem. The more your self-esteem increases, the more your life will improve, and the more capable you are of loving others.

Love and knowledge work in tandem. When you come from a place of love, your thirst for knowledge grows automatically. Gathering knowledge is key to cultivating healthy self-esteem. When you invest time gathering daily knowledge, on a daily basis, you set a marvelous example for your children of how love and knowledge can form an incredible strong foundation. Don't wait a moment longer to share this threshold with your children. Become a living example of what the power of love and knowledge together can do.

Pay attention to the children around you. They may be some of your best mentors. The quiet love of children has uplifted parents, teachers, friends and communities for countless years.

Once uplifted, the power of a loving parent rarely fails. Parents who put love into action reach greater heights and come far closer to fulfilling their highest potentials.

Every loving action a parent takes -whether taking their children to school, making breakfast, responding to their child's needs, developing family goals, or participating in family activities-is an action that will help maximize both their own and their children's potential as well.

Manifestations of Parents Lacking Love:
Parents who lack love usually:
- Display ungrateful and unforgiving attitudes
- Behave irresponsibly
- Do not effectively plan their days or organize their goals
- Are unclear about heir purpose in life

In addition, they often unknowingly reject the very knowledge that would provide solutions to improve their situations. Parents who lack love transfer these same negative emotions and behaviors to their children.

Characteristics of Loving Parents:
Loving parents:
- Do no wrong to others, and welcomes correction without being offended
- Quickly forgive the offenses of their children
- Demonstrate respect and honor as habitual behaviors
- Are deeply rooted and securely grounded
- Put their love in action by praying for those who dishonor or hurt them

Sayings of Loving Parents:
"I love myself, therefore I respect my time."

"I am a powerful channel of love. I receive love and give love easily and frequently."

"I attract loving and mutually beneficial friendships."

How to Build the Power of Love

Activities:
1. Forgive yourself for not having invested time wisely over the years to seek new knowledge daily
2. Forgive everyone who hurt you in the past. Do not allow another day to go by while you still hold on to an offense that has already stolen your purpose and vision, (letting go opens the door for you to add greater value to your family and your community)
3. Seek out a mentor or a coach who can assist you in maximizing your potential
4. Create a list of loving actions you would like to display to your family and surrounding community
5. Make a list of individuals you will positively impact through your loving actions _beginning today_
6. Keep a journal of the success you experience as you take these loving actions
7. Set intentions for daily self-growth activities

You deserve to be happy. Happiness is a choice. Forgiveness is also a choice. Take control of your life and demonstrate the power of love to your children, and your world, starting today.

Parents Self-Esteem Survey # 1

Your children bring home the following grades:

1.   English-A
2.   Math-F
3.   Music-B

Which grade deserves the most attention from you? Please select an answer.

Answer
_____

The correct answer is A. (English-A) Parents with healthy self-esteem
repeatedly pay more attention to their children's good grades first.
Proactively seeking solutions for correcting low grades will be their next step.

Parents Self-Esteem Development Exercise

1. What steps can you take today to add value to each family member?

2. What resources can you use to maximize your potential to experience the power of love every day, with _each _of your children?

3. What are some definite plans you will create to increase your ability to transfer love to others more powerfully?

4. How can you use the information you've learned about "The Power of Love" to empower your spouse and other adults who influence your children?

5. What is your first step? What action will you commit to taking _right now_ in order to improve your own self-esteem?

Affirmations for Building the Power of Love

I am a loving parent.

Love is my foundation.

I am rooted and grounded in love.

I demonstrate the power of love daily.

I choose to love myself.

I honor others.

I respect others.

I value my friendships.

I do everything with love.

My love never fails.

I forgive quickly.

My love is patient.

My love is kind.

My love is strong.

Power of Love Quotes

"A loving heart is the beginning of all knowledge." *(Thomas Carlyle)*

"A very small degree of hope is sufficient to cause the birth of love." *(Stendhal)*

"Being deeply loved by someone gives you strength, while loving someone deeply gives you courage." *(Lao Tzu)*

"I have found the paradox, if you love until it hurts, there can be no more hurt, only more love." *(Mother Teresa)*

"I like not only to be loved, but also to be told that I am loved." *(George Eliot)*

"If you want to be loved, be lovable." *(Ovid)*

"Let us always meet each other with a smile, for the smile is the beginning of love." *(Mother Teresa)*

"Love is all we have, the only way we can help each other." *(Euripides)*

"Love is an act of endless forgiveness, a tender look which becomes a habit." *(Peter Ustinov)*

"Love is the flower you 've go to let grow." ***(John Lennon)***

"Love is the foundation from which your decisions about your life should be made." ***(Darren L. Johnson)***

Kids' Purpose-Development Exercise

As early as the Elementary school level, you can help your children understand and know what they were born to accomplish. Developing purpose is very important for building healthy self-esteem.

Ask your children to write down the answers to these questions:

1. What makes you feel important to our family?

   _____

2. What makes you feel important to our community?

   _____

Ask your children to describe their personal purpose below in one sentence. (Use the space below provided.)

Example: *"My purpose in life is to share the power of love with my family and my community."*

(Child's Purpose Statement)

My purpose in life is to

_____

_____

Encourage your children to draw pictures showcasing their purpose!

Resources for Parents on the Subject of Love:

Suggested Books to Read for Younger Children:
-_Mama Do You Love Me?_ By Barbara Josse
-_Velveteen Rabbit_ by Margery Bianco

Suggested Books to Read for Older Children
-_Charlotte's Web_ by E.B. Wright
-_Lassie Come Home_ by Rosemary Wells

Suggested Books to Read for Parent:
-_365 Ways to Love Your Child_ by Caryl Krueger
-_Curriculum of Love_ by Morgan Daleo

Suggested Family Movies to Watch:
-"Sound of Music" (1965)—Julie Andrews
"-Free Willy" (1993) –Wincer, Richter

Healthy Self-Esteem grows as you effectively manage your personal purpose, vision, mission, priorities and values with excellence.

Secret # 2:
The Power of Joy

Story About Joy

Justin was a typical little boy who liked doing all sorts of things. He enjoyed going to school, except for "reading". It wasn't easy for Justin, so his assignments were always late, and when starting a new book he would give up in disgust.

One day Justin went to the bookstore with his grandfather and found, one that peaked his curiosity. He couldn't resist reading this book, so his grandfather purchased it for him. As usual, things didn't go well. He was about to quit after reading a couple of lines, when a character in the book began to speak to him.

"Psst! You aren't just going to leave me like this, are you? Come on! The least you can do is read with me a little longer". Justin was understandably shocked, but continued reading.

As he was using his imagination to being the character to life, it retorted, "Much better, now I can see myself, but what have you done to me? Arghh!"

Trying to make excuses, Justin replied, "I don't read very well."

The character interrupted him. "OK, no problem." Go on, read the last paragraph." I'm sure that if you try again, you'll do better. Justin took a deep breath. Using his imagination in a more fun and entertaining way, he began reading again, only this time with emotions.

"Hey! You forgot to stop at the end of the sentence!" prodded the character.

"Oh, yeah", responded Justin.

"Hmmm, I think I'm going to have to teach you how to read more fluidly so that you can do me justice", replied the character in its quick squeaky voice.

Although, almost paralyzed with fear, Justin began, reading the next paragraph, with ease and remembered to stop at the end of each sentence. Again, the character urged Justin to "Re-read the last sentence, but this time with more confidence; you make me sound like a whimp!"

After spending nearly the whole afternoon with this crazy new teacher, Justin did not want to stop reading. He had so much fun that he gave his new "instructor" a hearty "Thank You!" for having taught him how to read so well.

The character quickly replied, "But I didn't do anything, silly!' answered the character, in its usual quick manner. 'Don't you see that you've been practicing a lot, and enjoying it all the while? I bet that's the first time you've done that!'

Justin stopped to think. The truth was that previously, he read so poorly, because he had never practiced reading _for_ more than five minutes at a time. He had also always read angrily and grudgingly. Justin decided that without a doubt, the little character was correct. "OK, you're right, but thank you anyway," said Justin. Before he went to bed that night, he carefully placed his new book in his school bag.

The next morning Justin jumped out of bed and went running to retrieve his new book. He searched everywhere, but there was no sign of it. Although still sleepy, he was concerned and began franticly looking around the house. Worriedly, he began to wonder if he had spent the previous afternoon talking with the little character, or had simply dreamt the whole thing up. He decided to try and settle the matter by taking another book from his school bag, and reading it in character, just like he was taught.

Except for a couple of mispronunciations, it turned out not to be that bad after all. He imagined his bossy little teacher telling him to read more slowly, and that it looked like he was trying too hard. Justin gladly started over and began reading with confidence. He realized that the crazy little character had been right all along; it made no difference whether Justin had the magic book or not; he simply needed to keep practicing with confidence, in order to understand, and enjoy the process of reading.

From that day forward, Justin would imagine the characters urging him on, saying "Come on, my friend, where is the fun and excitement?" I can't come alive with you reading like this!"

Defining the Power of Joy:

Joy is the emotion of great delight or happiness caused by something exceptionally good or satisfying.

Joy builds strength and is based on truth. The power of joy comes from knowing who you are and why you were created.

By being "noble", (having a high moral and mental character of excellence), clears the path for attracting friendships that are honorable and joyful.

Most parents with healthy self-esteem invest significant time developing their moral and mental character. They know that doing so will help maximize their joyfulness.

Joy is not achieved through coincidence or by accident. It is achieved through a *process* of seeking things that are admirable, lovely, authentic, and pure. Joy is the result of choices associated with right thinking.

No matter how "hard" your day was parenting, know the hardship is temporary and joy will always return. Every day is a new day.

Moving forward, the wisdom gained from these "precious learning experiences" is foundational for growing joy beyond measure.

Manifestations of Parents Lacking Joy

Parents lacking joy are often:
- Easily irritated
- Impatient
- Emotionally off-balance
- Unhappy about everything

Many children have chosen to hurt themselves and others, when the lack of joy is transferred to them from an unhappy parent. Learning becomes a difficult task for children raised by joyless parents.

Characteristics of Joyful Parents:
Joyful parents:
- Manage their thoughts at all times
- Eliminate negative thinking
- Welcome authentic and pure thoughts without hesitation
- Laugh out loud
- Dance
- Enjoy life to its fullest

Sayings of a Joyful Parent:
"I am responsible for my own happiness."

"I enjoy seeking knowledge."

"I am happy with myself."

How to Build the Power of Joy

Activities:

1. Refuse to be controlled by negative emotions, and people who do not have good intentions for your development.
2. Wake up to new knowledge
3. Set your mind free from being a victim to people, things and situations
4. Create a list of 12 fun and exciting activities, one for each month.
5. Schedule time in your annual planner for activities and experiences which bring you joy
6. Welcome self-responsibility
7. Embrace the Power of Joy, as it will bring fulfillment to your life!

Parent Self-Esteem Survey # 2

Your child does the following:

( ) A. Disrespects his/her teacher
( ) B. Steals candy from the store
( ) C. Cleans his/her room daily

Which action deserves the most attention from you? Please select an answer.

Answer

The correct answer is C. (Clean his/her room daily –C)
Always pay the most attention to the behavior you would like to see your child repeat over and over.

Parent Self-Esteem Development Exercise

1. How will you use the power of joy to enhance your personal growth and move your development to a higher level?

2. What visual changes could you make to cultivate joyfulness in your home?

3. Do you have joyful stories you can share with your children? Schedule time to share them.

4. Could joy be a powerful tool for eliminating a "victim" mentality? Why/how?

5. Who do you admire that demonstrates joy in abundance? What traits do they exhibit that you could emulate in your own life?

Affirmations for Building the Power of Joy

I am a joyful parent.

I gain strength when I am joyful.

I choose to be joyful.

I share joyful experiences with others.

I manage my emotions.

I am very happy.

I enjoy being successful.

I rejoice in all things.

There is joy deep in my heart.

I am happy to be alive.

I shout for joy daily.

Strength and joy belong to me.

All the joy I need is within me NOW!

Power of Joy Quotes

"Joy in looking and comprehending is nature's most beautiful gift." **(Albert Einstein)**

"We are shaped by our thoughts; we become what we think. When the mind is pure, joy follows like a shadow that never leaves." **(Buddha)**

"Joy is a net of love by which you can catch souls." **(Mother Teresa)**

"Since you get more joy out of giving joy, you should put a good deal of thought into the happiness you are able to give." **(Eleanor Roosevelt)**

"Your success and happiness lies in you. Resolve to keep happy, and your joy and you shall form an invincible host against difficulties." **(Helen Keller)**

"There is joy in work. There is no happiness except in the realization that we have accomplished something." **(Henry Ford)**

"The walls we build around us to keep sadness out also keeps out joy." **(Jim Rohn)**

"Worry never robs tomorrow of it's sorrow, it only saps today of it's joy." **(Leo Buscaglia)**

"The bond that links your true family is not one of blood, but of respect and joy in each other's life." **(Richard Bach)**

Kids Vision Development Exercise

Vision provides direction for children and helps them operate in a healthy and powerful state of mind.

Activity: Use these questions to help your child create a personal vision statement that moves them toward their destiny and building healthy self-esteem.

1. What big goal will inspire you toward greatness?

   _____

2. How good do you want to be at this goal?

   _____

Ask your child to write their personal vision statement below in one sentence.

Example: My vision is to inspire my family and friends by being a person with healthy self-esteem.

(Child's vision statement)

My vision in life is to

_____

_____

Encourage your children to draw pictures
showcasing their personal vision.

Resources for Parents on the Subject of Joy:

Suggested Books to Read for Younger Children:
-*Treasury for Children* by James Herriot
-*Berenstain Bears: The Joy of Giving* by Jan Berenstain

Suggested Books to Read for Older Children:
-*Story of Ferdinand* by Munroe Leaf
-*The Other Wise Man* by Henry Van Dyke

Suggested Books to Read for Parents:
-*The Secret of a Joy filled life* by Tommy Newberry
-*Joy: The Happiness that Comes From Within* by Osho

Suggested Family Movies to Watch:
-*"Mary Poppins"* (1964)---Julie Andrews
-*"Willy Wonka and the Chocolate Factory"* (1971) –
Gene Widler

Children with low self-esteem are reactive. They always complain, blame others, and are easily offended.

Children with healthy self-esteem are proactive. They are self-disciplined, listen attentively, and look for solutions.

Secret # 3:
The Power of Peace

Story About Peace

Once upon a time an old woman had lost her husband and lived alone. Her entire life she had worked so hard as a housekeeper, but misfortunes had left her in bankruptcy, and now she was so old and was unable to work. As she got older, she found it harder and harder to do things: Her hand trembled making it harder to hold on to things. She couldn't walk up and down the stairs without gasping for breadth. Her vision was so impaired that when cooking a meal, she wasn't able to read a recipe or put the right ingredients together to cook a meal. Daily, the majority of her hours were spent worrying about how she could help herself.

Her three grown boys had long since moved out and gotten married. They were so busy with their own lives, that they barely had time to eat dinner with their mother once a week (maybe).

As the old woman become more and more frail, seemly her children visited her less and less. She glumly thought to herself, "They do not want to be with me now," because they're afraid that I will become a burden to them."

One night, she again lay awake unable to sleep. She kept wondering what would become of her, so she devised a plan to support herself. The following morning she activated her plan and went to see her friend next door. She discovered that sharing the "plan" with her neighbor made her feel better about her situation. She asked if her neighbor would help her keep the house clean. Next, the old woman went to see a different friend from church. She asked her to help with cooking meals. After sharing the "plan" again, she felt even more optimistic about her circumstances.

Finally, she went to see the local baker, and asked him if he would help her baked cookies for the holidays. All the way home she smiled with excitement from the bakers response. More and more her outlook improved. She began cleaning up her house, baked some more delicious cookies and made preparations for the next day. There was a new found calm that emanated outward from her.

The next time her children came to visit, they immediately noticed that there was something different about their mother. They were in awe of the new positive changes: how well their mother looked, and how she had taken such good care of her home. As the smell of delicious and tasty cookies wafted through the house, her children asked, "What is that alluring smell mother"? The old woman replied, "Oh, that's another batch of cookies from the local bakery."

"The local bakery?" asked her astonished children. "Yes", replied the old woman." Her children pressed further, "why would they bake cookies for you?" The old woman began to tell them about her loneliness, and how it motivated her to find a solution. She told her children "I had no idea feeling sorry for myself, pushed people away." Her children asked her to explain. The old woman said, "I was so unhappy with my life, and imagined what would happen if I simply waited for my children to help me." Her children drew closer to hear more about this "plan" that had changed her life.

The old woman continued, "All these years, I have worked very hard to raise my children with dignity and respect. Unfortunately, I only forgot one very important thing." Her children queried, "What was that mom?" Smiling from ear to ear, in a calm and loving voice, she replied," I forgot to add peace that surpasses all understanding to my daily routine." The children continued to listen intently.

As she shared more details of the "plan" with her children, they watched the glow of peace and calm overtake their mother's face more and more. In complete awe of their mother's transformation, the children asked if they could share the "plan" with their own families, neighbors and friends.

The three boys silently looked at each other and smiled. They knew that they had just been given one of the greatest gifts a parent could pass on to their children: the life changing "power of peace".

Secret # 3: The Power of Peace

Defining the Power of Peace:

Peace is a serene, tranquil state of mind that is without conflict. Peaceful parents create an atmosphere of safe, and confident trust, which in turn leads to a calm and steady "present-moment" focus.

Peaceful parents also tend to have more positive outlooks and actively look for the good in their days. They are masters at managing their thoughts. Their optimism makes it easy for them to reject negative ones. Peaceful parents have a much higher propensity to produce peaceful children.

Operating in an atmosphere of confidence increases a child's productivity. Peaceful children find it much easier to complete assignments, chores, and activities with far less effort. Good grades, successful friendships and loving experiences await children whose parents have mastered this powerful secret.

Both peaceful parents and peaceful children also tend to have larger, more precise vocabularies. With an advanced ability to communicate, children are better problem-solvers and suffer from fewer social, behavioral, and emotional difficulties. (For some great ideas to help your child build their vocabulary, see http://www.childdevelopmentinfo.com/learning/vocabulary.shtml).

Manifestations of Parents Lacking Peace:

Parents lacking peace usually:

- Earn lower salaries
- Are deficient in problem-solving abilities
- Have emotional difficulties
- Are tormented by limited and negative thinking

Characteristics of Peaceful Parents:

Many peaceful parents:

- Invest the first thirty minutes of each day to planning it
- Get plenty of rest
- Drink lots of water
- Start their day with a healthy and balanced breakfast
- Manage their time wisely
- Reduce stress and increase productivity

Sayings of Peaceful Parents:

"I plan my day for tomorrow before I go to bed tonight."

"Understanding my priorities for each day calms my mind."

"Everything works out for my good because my day is organized."

How to Build the Power of Peace

Activities:

1. Write down the names of individuals who increase your peace.
2. Create a thirty-day plan for adding value to these individuals.
3. Observe your thoughts. If you find them to be negative or limiting, stop and replace them with positive ones.
4. Focus on the positive. You attract what you dwell on.
5. Consciously turn your attention to exactly those things you want to attract into your life.
6. If you are surrounded with turmoil, deliberately take 90 seconds to visualize a setting that is calm, and tranquil. As your own mood improves, you will find more peace.
7. Reduce clutter and increase your level of organization. As your physical and mental spaces become clear, greater peace will be an inevitable result.

Parent Self-Esteem Survey # 3

Your child's teacher does the following:

( ) A. Screams at your child

( ) B. Pays your child a compliment

( ) C. Ignores your child

Which action deserves the most attention from you? Please select an answer.

Answer

The correct answer is **B**. Consciously pay the most attention to the behavior you would like to see others demonstrate with your child.

Parents Self-Esteem Development Exercise

1. Set aside at least 15 minutes each day to plan for the next 24 hours.

2. Decide on your three family priorities for the next 24 hours. List the specific actions you can take to move toward each priority. Commit to taking at least one step toward each priority every day.

3. Spend time thinking about this question: "What will it take to increase my performance level?"

4. Identify obstacles. What are some possible interruptions to your personal peaceful atmosphere? Visualize yourself successfully eliminating them.

5. Set aside time for two 5-minute "clutter-busting sessions" every day. They will be nice breaks from your regular routines. *Where* you start doesn't matter. It could be in your home, office, car, garage, wallet or purse. Every small bit of clutter you remove from your life will bring you one step closer to personal peace.

Affirmations for Building the Power of Peace

I am a peaceful parent.

I surround myself with a peaceful atmosphere.

I manage and control all negative thoughts.

I plan and organize my day ahead of time.

I actively remove clutter from my life.

I focus on my priorities first.

I value my time.

I am always on time for appointments.

I organize and manage my family goals for each day.

I live in a peaceful state of mind.

I use a weekly assignment management list.

I use a "Time Management Planner" daily.

I follow a monthly organizational chart.

I listen to music that calms my mind.

Power of Peace Quotes

"If we have no peace, it is because we have forgotten we belong to each other." **(Mother Teresa)**

"It isn't enough to talk about peace. One must believe in it. And it isn't enough to believe in it. One must work at it." **(Eleanor Roosevelt)**

"Nobody can bring you peace but yourself." **(Ralph Waldo Emerson)**

"Of one thing I am certain, the body is not the measure of healing, peace is." **(Phyllis McGinley)**

"One cannot subdue a man by holding back his hands. Lasting peace comes not from force." **(David Borenstein)**

"Peace is the first thing the angels sang." **(John Keble)**

"The most valuable possession you can own is an open heart. The most powerful weapon you can be is an instrument of peace." **(Carlos Santana)**

"The quest for peace begins in the home, in the school and in the workplace." **(Silvia Cartwright)**

"Those who are at war with others are not at peace with themselves." **(William Hazlitt)**

"You cannot find peace by avoiding life." **(Virginia Woolf)**

Kids Mission Development Exercise

Your children's mission statement is an effective
tool to help him/her stay focused on the benefits
of serving others without being selfish.

Coach your children in answering the following questions:

1. What is the best contribution you make to
   your parents and family members?

   _____

2. How do you serve the community? (Do
   you volunteer at your school, church or
   temple?)

   _____

**Write your personal mission statement
below in one sentence.**

Example: My mission is to add value to my
family, friends and community.

(Child's Mission Statement)

My mission in life is to

_____

_____

Draw a picture showcasing your child's mission!

Resources for Parents on the Subject of Peace:

Suggested Books to Read for Younger Children:
-_Wangari's Trees of Peace_ by Jeanette Winter
-_The Peace Book_ by Todd Parr

Suggested Books to Read for Older Children:
-_Enjoying True Peace_ by Stephanie Perry Moore
-_Amazing Peace_ by Maya Angelou

Suggested Books to Read for Parents:
-_10 Secrets for Success and Inner Peace_ by Wayne Dwyer
-_The Voice of Knowledge_ by Janet Mills

Suggested Family Movies to Watch:
-"The Peace"! (2005)---Harry Belafonte
-"Pilgrim of Peace" (2004) –Mahatma Ghandi

Children with healthy self-esteem identify distress as an opportunity for growth and development.

Secret # 4:
The Power of Patience

Story About Patience

Rebecca was a brave young girl, who dreamed of becoming the best ballerina in the world. There wasn't a single person in the whole school who danced with as much poise as she did. Rebecca hoped to become head of the dance group and replace the cowardly ballerina who was currently taking charge. The teacher liked Rebecca, but was a bit shock to hear about her ambition to be a "lead" ballerina.

"Your desire is sincere, but I'm afraid it can't happen right now. You still have much to learn," said the teacher.

That was the worst thing that she could have said. Furious, Rebecca, stormed out of her dance class, and was determined to learn all there was to know about becoming a "prima ballerina". Angrily, she thought to herself, "I _WILL_ be the best ballerina at my school!"

Rebecca asked several family members lots of questions and read all kind of books, but didn't learn any new "secrets". One day, she got the opportunity to meet a very special friend of her mother's. This family friend had been a professional ballerina whose story was featured in the national newspapers.

During their conversation, Rebecca learned that this woman owned and operated a dance studio for children. Even more determined to be a "lead ballerina" at her school, Rebecca skillfully plotted how she would convince her mom to enroll her in this dance program.

She was successful and began classes' right afterschool the following week. Before the first class started, Rebecca was asked to turn in her own ballet shoes.

"You won't be needing those any more because you'll be getting better ones," said her new dance teacher. Rebecca handed her the shoes, which were immediately throw into the garbage. A serious, old woman of few words, then escorted Rebecca to her place on the dance floor.

As she walked away, the instructor said, "Your training will begin in an hour." An hour?! At first Rebecca thought this was a joke, but soon realized that the old woman wasn't kidding. For the first five minutes, Rebecca nervously tried all manner of silly tactics to try to get the training to begin. Unsuccessful, Rebecca ended having to wait the full hour, but enjoyed every minute in spite of herself.

As promised, the first lesson began precisely at one minute of the hour. "You have just learned the first "secret" to being a "lead" ballerina. Patience is the first skill that all ballerinas must master before becoming the best that they could be." Rebecca chuckled as the old woman went on to remind her of all the crazy stunts she had pulled out of impatience. "Now you're ready to learn how to dance with "greatness." Rebecca smiled and had to admit that her new dance teacher was right.

Secret # 4: The Power of Patience

Defining the Power of Patience:
A patient person is one who is quiet, steady, and even-tempered when faced with delays, negative circumstances, or long-term difficulties.

The Power of Patience is something parents will need in order to endure the inevitable difficulties with their children, family members, friends, (and sometimes even with themselves!). The ability to endure hardships without complaining is truly powerful.

If you are a parent, you are already familiar with the abundant opportunities to develop the power of patience, right? There is no better opportunity to grow in patience than through a child!

Nor do the lessons get easier: as children get older, parents need _more_ patience to deal with higher levels of trials, tribulations, and hardships. The teen years can be an excellent time for parents to truly understand the power that comes with "counting it all joy." (Yes, I had to smile as I wrote that.)

Parents with healthy self-esteem allow plenty of room for patience with their children. When well modeled, children are then enabled to build their own inner strength and strong self-esteem: a perfect result.

A steadfast and patient child will persist through the difficulties involved with developing virtues that enable them to be winners in life.

For most of us however, afflictions may be the greatest test of our patience. All of us are subject to events or circumstances that are hard to bear.

When we face sickness, pain, grief, or loss, our mastery (or lack) of patience becomes immediately obvious. Nothing reveals our true strengths or weaknesses like the anxiety, tension, and frustration that can be brought on by such events.

Knowing deep within your heart that trials are necessary to master patience is definitely the key, which unlocks our ability to handle life's stresses and attain true peace of mind.

Manifestations of Parents Lacking Patience

Parents lacking patience are often:
- In a hurry
- Agitated
- Frustrated
- Intolerant
- Angry
- Restless
- More prone to violence

Characteristics of a Patient Parent:

Patient parents:
- Practice humility
- Embrace hope
- Manage their life skillfully
- Endure all things
- Cultivate inner strength with joy
- Remain steadfast

Sayings of a Patient Parent:

"I am in no hurry."

"There is plenty of time."

"No trials or hardships have power over me."

How to Build the Power of Patience

Activities:

1. See if you can spot the "triggers" that cause you to lose your patience.
2. As you list all the things that cause you anxiety, tension, or frustration, look for underlying realities that you have a hard time accepting.
3. If you can't change those realities, just "let them go."
4. Make an effort to be more patient in short-term, inconsequential situations (like waiting in line at the bank). The better you become at handling the smaller "issues," the more strength you will gain for more difficult situations.
5. Practice gratitude.
6. Situations, which try your patience, also bring you opportunities for personal growth. Try being "fascinated" rather than "frustrated."
7. Focus on what matters most. There are only a handful of things that really matter in life. Impatience results when we take our eyes *off* of those things that matter the most.

Parent Self-Esteem Survey # 4

Your spouse does the following:

( ) A. Complains about your parenting style

( ) B. Compliments you

( ) C. Disrespects you

Which action deserves the most attention from you? Please select an answer.

Answer

The correct answer is **B**. Insist on paying the most attention to the behavior you would like to see your spouse repeat over and over.

Parent Self Esteem Development Exercise

1. What are some areas you need to work on with respect to becoming more patient?

2. How will you benefit by being more patient?

3. What will it do for your relationships with your children if you are more patient with them?

4. Create a list of the people you need to practice being more patient with. Pick one and start practicing!

5. Create a scrap page with the words "I AM PATIENT" in the center. Add pictures of people or situations you need to be

more patient with. Review the page every morning and evening for six-weeks.

6. Write down your experiences after 7 days and share them with a close friend. Was the activity useful? If so, add this activity to your planner and share it with your child.

Affirmations for Building the Power of Patience

I am a patient parent.

I choose to be patient.

I will persist until I succeed.

I am hopeful.

No weapons formed against me will prosper.

All I need is within me NOW.

I eat trials and tribulations for breakfast.

I humble myself during times of affliction.

I gladly seek counsel from others.

I solve my problems with ease.

I am not afraid.

I believe everything will always work out for my good.

I am strong inside and outside.

Nothing has the power to destroy me without my permission.

Power of Patience Quotes

"A man who is master of patience is a master of everything else." **(George Savile)**

"Deliberately seek opportunities for kindness, sympathy, and patience." **(Evelyn Underhill)**

"Endurance is patience concentrated." **(Thomas Carlyle)**

"For anything worth having one must pay the price; and the price is always work, patience, love self-sacrifice-no paper currency, no promises to pay, but the gold of real service." **"John Burroughs"**

"Genius is eternal patience." **(Michelangelo)**

"Good ideas are not adopted automatically. They must be driven into practice with courageous patience." **(Hyman Rickover)**

"Have patience with all things, But, first of all with yourself." **(Saint Francis de Sales)**

"I have just three things to teach: simplicity, patience, compassion. These three are your greatest treasures." **(Lao Tzu)**

"Patience can't be acquired overnight. It is just like building up a muscle. Everyday you need to work on it." **(Eknath Easwaran)**

Kids Values Development Exercise

Healthy values provide solid foundations for children. A child
with strong values tends to be a child with better behaviors.
(Help your children answer the following questions.)

1. What does it mean to be patient? Can you
   give an example?

   _____

2. When is it hardest for you to be patient?

   _____

3. What does it mean when someone says
   "No"?

   _____

(Explain the difference between making a request and making a
demand, and what the consequences are. Also explain that when
you do say "no", sometimes it is about "waiting" rather than
never having or doing what they've asked for.)

Resources for Parents on the Subject of Patience:

Suggested Books to Read for Younger Children:
-<u>Sammy's Gadget Galaxy</u> by Michael Waite
-<u>It's Taking Too Long</u> by Cheryl Wagner

Suggested Books to Read for Older Children:
-<u>A Little Book of Inner Strength</u> by Eknath Easwaran
-<u>Chicken Soup for the Teenage Soul</u> by Jack Canfield

Suggested Books to Read for Parents:
-<u>7 Spiritual Gifts for Waiting</u> by Holly Whitcomb
-<u>Living Beyond Yourself</u> by Beth Moore

Suggested Family Movies to Watch:
-"Dream Girls" (2006)---Beyonce Knowles
-"The Sound of Music" (2010) –Julie Andrews

Children with healthy self-esteem are choice-motivated which builds independence and self-responsibility.

Secret # 5:
The Power of Kindness

Story About Kindness

For centuries, "Goliath the Giant" had lived in "The Cave of Hostility". Giants had been peaceful and isolated beings up until when "King Henry the Horrible" accused them of ruining the kingdom's harvest and ordered all the giants be hunted down. Goliath was the only giant that survived. After that, he became the most violent creature there had ever been. He was too powerful to be defeated by anyone who dared to enter his cave. Regardless of how brave or powerful they were, a deadly fate was always suffered.

Future Kings were embarrassed by Henry the Horrible's behavior and tried in vain to make peace with Goliath. His hostility and violent anger, would cause him to do away with every human being he came into contact with, without listening to what they had to say. There was a beautiful treasure inside Goliath's cave, so many adventurers and warriors came from all over the world to try to steal it. Even though the king left him alone, Goliath's hatred for humans continued to grow as strong as ever.

One day, a deadly snake from the swamps bit a young princess, and only the giants knew a secret potion to make the antidote. Thus, the King had sent his best soldiers and bravest warriors to beg for Goliath's help. The king promised them that if one were successful, they could marry the princess. However, neither their shields, their most powerful weapons, or their well-polished armor could do anything to squelch of Goliath's rage.

The King continued to ask for help throughout the kingdom, this time not only promising the princess's hand, with offering riches and the protection of the best skilled warriors, to any person willing to accept.

Embarking on the quest, many subjects were armed in all sorts of different ways, (including an invisible sword), and protected by the best warriors. Every last one of them failed. As the king began to give up all hope, a young musician armed only with a harp volunteered. "I want to change into a beautiful flower and have the voice of an angel", he pleaded to the warrior with the invisible sword. His request was granted, and so there appeared, at the cave entrance, an extraordinary beautiful flower, which was singing a lovely tune to the sound of a harp.

Upon hearing something so different than the ugly clanking of weapons, shields, and armor, Goliath's hostility started to soften. As the flower kept singing, he took the flower in his hand, so he would be able to hear it better. The song it sang was about the story of a young princess close to death, who could only be saved by a good-hearted giant.

The song was so moving, that it caused Goliath to listen with great compassion. As he became more calm and tranquil, the flower felt it was safe enough to stop singing. In a normal speaking voice, he foretold about the princess's impending demise, and that the king wanted to come to a fair and lasting peace agreement with Goliath.

Believing in the truth of what the flower told him, tired of so much fighting, and leaving the cave (and his hostility) behind, Goliath quickly went to save the princess. The young musician not only won the princess's hand, but all the hearts in the kingdom as well. He then became the best King to ever rule the land.

Secret # 5: The Power of Kindness

Defining the Power of Kindness:

To be kind is to be a person who has a good and giving nature and who is considerate, helpful, forgiving, gentle, loving, and affectionate.

A parent with the power of kindness will always find favor with their children, spouse, and (nearly) everyone that they come into contact with. Life becomes easier to manage, because being kind allows us to be better communicators, have more compassion with ourselves, and impact others in positive ways.

On the surface, kindness seems like an easy thing to achieve but for some of us kindness can be harder than we think. Most of us find it easy enough to be kind to those who are kind to us, but it is much more difficult to be kind to people we don't know or who hurt us in some way. Fortunately, being kind is a habit or discipline we can choose to achieve.

Remember that everyone has life challenges: hardships, sadness, disappointments, and loss. Remember this quote from Plato: "Be kind, for everyone you meet is fighting a hard battle."

When you are tempted to "react" to another person in a negative way, stop and ask yourself this question: "Will this reaction be kind?" If your answer is "No," it is a good reminder to change your action before you do or say something you will later regret.

When someone acts unkindly to you, remember this: their action may have nothing to do with you personally…it may simply be a result of their own frustration, anger, or upset from something else in their life. The greatest kindness you can show may be to just withhold judgment.

The more you master the art and practice of kindness, the more empowered you become to love your enemies and those who speak negatively about you. Healthy personal self-esteem can actually allow you to share words of compassion with those who are unkind.

Observe kind people. You will often see them take an action that will be completely unexpected: they will forgive the other person! Kindness is a choice. Caring for others, our environment (including animals and plants!), and ourselves is a wonderful way to live our lives.

Parents, here's one more reminder: What you model for your children has enormous impact. As you model kindness toward your enemies and those who speak negatively about you, you will be empowering your children to do the same.

Being kind to others not only increases your own self-esteem, it also helps to increase your child's potential, productivity, stability, and security. What a blessing!

Manifestations of Parents Lacking Kindness:
Parents lacking kindness are:
- Usually impatient with their children's learning development
- Speak to their children's mistakes
- Entertain shallow relationships

Characteristics of Kind Parents
Parents of Kindness often:
- Encourage their children and other family members
- Are insightful about their children's potential
- Explore ideas for adding value to others
- Use their imagination for touching the heart of people

Sayings of a Kind Parent:

"Thank you."

"I have a sound and generous mind."

"I enjoy being kind to others."

How to Build the Power of Kindness

Activities:

1. Create a list of family members that shared their love and kindness with you throughout the year.

2. Write letters thanking them for doing so. Let them know how their actions have inspired you to be the best you can be in the coming year.

3. Show kindness through loving animals and the living world.

4. Kindness isn't restricted to just caring about our fellow humans. Loving and respecting all living species is an expression of deep kindness.

5. Care for yourself. Kindness is a choice. Why not _choose_ to be kind and forgiving toward yourself? You are worthy of receiving kindness too!

6. Realize that the impacts of kindness are like the ripples in a pond when you toss in a stone. You never know how a single act of kindness may touch someone or inspire them to "pass it on."

7. Be the catalyst. Start the ripples moving.

Parent Self-Esteem Survey # 5

Your neighbor does the following:

(   ) A. Made your family cookies
(   ) B. Got angry at you
(   ) C. Refused to speak to you

Which action deserves the most attention from you? Please select an answer.

Answer

The correct answer is **A**. Always pay the most attention to the behavior you would like to see your neighbor repeat over and over...the *kind* behavior.

Parent Self Esteem Development Exercise

1. How can you use the information learned about kindness to improve your personal self-esteem?

2. What are the benefits of activating the power of kindness in your life?

3. List three specific things you can do in the next 24 hours to show kindness. DO them before this time tomorrow.

4. Purchase a bouquet or two of fresh flowers. Visit a local nursing home with your child. Ask permission to visit the residents, to share fresh flowers with them, and to share a kind word with them.

5. Think of a specific way you can demonstrate the power of kindness to your child's teachers. Take action on that idea right away.

Affirmations for Building the Power of Kindness

I enjoy sharing.

I choose to be kind to myself and others.

I enjoy being kind to my children.

I demonstrate the power of kindness effortlessly.

All the kindness I need is within me NOW.

I practice kindness daily.

I think only thoughts of kindness toward myself and others.

I enjoy giving to my family.

My life is filled with kindness.

I attract kind people into my life.

As I am kind to others, kindness comes back to me.

I am always thinking of new ways to show kindness to others.

Kindness is just naturally part of my character.

I gladly share my time and volunteer to help others.

Power of Kindness Quotes

"Kindness is the language which the deaf can hear and the blind can see." **(Mark Twain)**

"Kindness, like a boomerang, always return." **(Author Unknown)**

"Real generosity is doing something nice for someone who will never find out." **(Frank A. Clark)**

"We have two ears and one mouth so we can listen twice as much as we speak." **(Epictetus)**

"Being considerate of others will take your children farther in life than a college degree." **(Marian Wright Edelman)**

"Make it a practice to judge person and things in the most favorable light at all times and under all circumstances." **(Saint Vincent de Paul)**

"A person who is nice to you, but rude to the waiter, is not a nice person." **(Dave Barry)**

"Life is short, but there is always time for courtesy." **(Ralph Waldo Emerson)**

"One man cannot hold another man in the ditch without remaining down in the ditch with him." **(Booker T. Washington)**

"The true meaning of life is to plant trees, under whose shade you do not expect to sit." **(Nelson Mandela)**

Kids Kindness Development Exercise

When children practice small acts of kindness, with time those acts develop into larger acts of compassion. Children also develop greater self-esteem because it is impossible to be kind to others and not have kindness reflect back onto us. (Assist your child with the completion of this worksheet.)

A.   Write down 2 kind things you will do within the next 24 hours.

1. _____

2. _____

B.   Choose 3 things to do from this list and cross them off after you do them.

1. Smile at someone your age you've never met before.
2. Give someone a compliment. (For example, "I love your t-shirt!")
3. Offer to help someone even if they haven't asked you for help.

4. Say "Hello" to someone before they say "Hello" to you.
5. Share something you have with someone else.

Resources for Parents on the Subject of Kindness:

Suggested Books to Read for Younger Children:
-_Kids Random Acts of Kindness_ by Conari Press
-_Practice Random Acts of Kindness_ by Will Glennon

Suggested Books to Read for Older Children:
-_Acts of Kindness_ by Meladee McCarty
-_Pay It Forward_ by Catherine Ryan Hyde

Suggested Books to Read for Parents:
-_Bringing Up Moral Children_ by A. Lynn Scoresby

Suggested Family Movies to Watch:
-"Precious" (2010)---Gabourey Sidibe
-"Joshua" (2001)---Tony Goldwyn

Children with healthy self-esteem are skilled at identifying multiple options for solving personal problems.

Secret # 6:
The Power of Goodness

Story About Goodness

There once was a girl who was very wealthy and self-centered. She had virtually everything a girl could ever want, but she was only interested in the most rare and curious objects. While shopping at the market, she convinced her parents to buy a very old and mysterious mirror. After brining it home, the girl admired herself and noticed that she looked very unhappy. She tried smiling and making funny faces, but her expression remained the same.

Surprised, the girl went off to buy some sweets and came back as happy as could be. She again peered into the mirror, but her image was still sad-looking. She then bought all kinds of candy, toys and old junk, but her reflection remained unchanged. Fed up, the girl deliberately hid the mirror in a corner.

"Jumping Jupiter, what a horrible mirror! It's the first time I've seen a mirror that didn't work correctly!', she quipped.

That same afternoon she went out into the street to play. Quickly bored, she made her way to the store where a little boy who was crying his heart out. She was so distraught, that she went over to comfort him, and see what had happened. "I've lost my parents and am very lonely," said the little boy.

Together the two set off in search of his parents. As he wouldn't stop crying, the little girl spent all of her money on buying candy to cheer him up. Finally, after much walking, they successfully found the little boy's parents who were out looking for him, and very worried.

After a happy reunion, the little girl said good-bye and walked off toward the park. It was getting late, so she decided to turn around and head for home. She went to her room, and immediately noticed a shinning light coming from the same corner she had placed the mirror in. As she got closer and looked at her reflection, she realized that the light was coming directly from inside her own body.

The little girl now understood the "mystery" of that mirror; the only mirror which could faithfully reflect the true happiness level of its owner. She realized it was accurate and authentic, because she felt happy from having helped that little boy.

And every morning since then, when the little girl looks in that mirror and fails to see a special shine, she already knows what she has to do to bring it back again.

Secret # 6: The Power of Goodness

Defining the Power of Goodness:

Goodness is choosing to live in moral excellence. The strength of a parent's goodness toward their family and others, is an excellent indicator of their level of core self-esteem.

In a sense, "goodness" is a like a seal of approval and a healthy level of esteem that follows people who manage themselves responsibly. A responsible parent is one who has mastered his or her emotions, *has* high standards of moral excellence, and exhibits generosity.

Parents who exhibit the power of goodness give their children a strong foundation with a solid base. Children who are rooted and grounded in the power of parents who share goodness are children who attract success.

One of the simplest (but not necessarily the easiest!) ways to live a life characterized by goodness, is to love others and treat them as we would like to be treated. This is a high standard of living that takes discipline and self-control.

Interestingly, being "good" is measured both by what you *don't do* (harm others, for example), and by what you *do* (thinking of others before yourself, for instance).

Cultivating goodness is a personal developmental goal that parents should actively pursue. Every parent (and every person for that matter!) has the potential and ability to demonstrate the power of goodness at any time. Goodness is an important step on the road to success and happiness. It is a powerful secret to healthy self-esteem!

Manifestations of Parents Lacking the Power of Goodness:
Parents lacking goodness often criticize their children's performance, and *fail to* give needed encouragement and praise. Children raised by these parents often develop a fear of *success*, and refuse to persist in self-improvement when they encounter obstacles.

Characteristics of Parents with the Power of Goodness
Parents full of goodness:
- Manage themselves responsibly.
- Are generous and trustworthy.
- Discipline themselves to set goals.
- Treat others as they would like to be treated.

Sayings of Parents with the Power of Goodness:
"I am responsible."
"I discipline myself toward excellence."
"I choose to embrace goodness in every area of my life."

How to Build the Power of Goodness

Activities:
1. Write down a list of behaviors that are associated with the power of goodness. Create a plan that will allow you to practice each behavior. Complete the plan within the next 6-12 months.
2. Make a list of your role models, then answer these questions:
    a. Why do I look up to these people?
    b. How are they making the world a better place? (Can I do the same?)
    c. What are their best qualities? (How can I incorporate those qualities into my own life?)
3. Accept everyone as your brothers and sisters no matter what their age, race, or culture.
4. Do something good for someone else every day.

Parent Self-Esteem Survey # 6

Your child did the following:

( ) A. Broke a glass

( ) B. Made you breakfast

( ) C. Helped a neighbor

Which actions deserve the most attention from you? Please select an answer(s).

Answer

The correct answers are **B and C**. Always pay the most attention to the behaviors you would like to see your child repeat over and over.

Parents Self-Esteem Development Exercise

1. What are some ideas for increasing the power of goodness in your life?

2. How can your goodness help your children?

3. What motivates your behaviors of goodness?

4. What goals do you want to accomplish with the power of goodness?

5. What books can you read to continue developing your self-esteem?

Affirmations for Building the Power of Goodness

I choose to live a life of moral goodness.

I speak the truth to my children.

I keep my promises to my children.

I demonstrate goodness every day.

I cultivate goodness in my life.

My deepest desire is to share the power of goodness.

I pursue goodness with passion.

I am connected with the power of goodness.

I control my negative emotions and behavior.

When I act from goodness, I attract goodness.

I am inspired by my child's goodness.

Goodness is my passion.

My goodness comes from deep within my heart.

Kids Thought Development Exercise

Children who are unable to manage their thoughts are unable to manage their behavior. (Assist your child with completing this assignment)

1. What does it mean to be good? List two things you could do to be good to others in the family.

   1. _____

   2. _____

2. Who do you know outside your family that you could be good to today? List two specific things you will do for them today.

   1. _____

   2. _____

Draw a picture showcasing your new thoughts

Power of Goodness Quotes

"Goodness and hard work are rewarded with respect."
(Luther Campbell)

"Goodness is the only investment that never fails."
(Henry David Thoreau)

"It is a great mistake to think of great without goodness and I pronounce it as certain that there never was a truly great man who was not at the same time truly virtuous."
(Benjamin Franklin)

"Man has two great spiritual needs. One for forgiveness. The other one is for goodness." **(Billy Graham)**

"Never esteem men on account of their riches or station. Respect goodness, find it where you may." **(William Cobbett)**

"Of all the dignities of the mind, goodness is the greatest, being the character of the Diety; and without it, man is a busy, mischievous, and wretched thing." **(Francis Bacon)**

"Our awesome responsibility to ourselves, to our children, and to the future is to create ourselves in the image of goodness, because the future depends on the nobility of our imaginings." **(Barbara Grizzuti Harrison)**

Resources for Parents on the Subject of Goodness:

Suggested Books to Read for Younger Children:
-*The Honest to Goodness Truth* by Patricia McKissack
-*Any Small Goodness* by Tony Johnston

Suggested Books to Read for Older Children:
-*Goodness Graces* by Diana Jenkins
-*Thank You* by Anna Krusinski

Suggested Books to Read for Parents:
-*20 Teachable Virtues* by Jerry Wychoff

Suggested Family Movies to Watch:
-"*It's a Wonderful World*" (1947)---James Stewart
-"*A Christmas Story*" (1983)---Melinda Dillion

Children with a healthy self-esteem have a strong desire to add value to themselves, their family and their community.

Secret # 7:
The Power of Optimism

Story About Optimism

Mark Taylor was a pre-teen boy who was never happy with anything. He had lots of friends, and parents, who loved him dearly, but all Mark could think about was what he didn't have, or the things he did have which he didn't like. If his parents offered him a ride to visit his friends, he would complain that the car was too big or too slow. If he went to the zoo, he'd come back disappointed because they hadn't let him feed the lions. If he played football with his friends, he would complained, that there were too many of them for just one ball....

One day, Mark was caught off guard by a cloud named, "Sophie the prankster". While drifting past, she had heard all of Mark's complaining, and wafted over to see who could possibly be so negative? When Sophie was directly above Mark, she showered him with bright orange rain, (that was Sophie's favorite trick to play on grumpy old pre-teens).

Mark wasn't at all impressed by this new development, and it just made him complain even more. After almost two weeks, he realized he couldn't get away from the cloud.

The only one who had been willing to hang around with Mark during all those bright orange and rainy days was a happy and generous girl named Stephanie. All the other children would run off to avoid getting soaked and ending up completely orange. One day, when Mark was at the end of his rope, Stephanie said to him: "Cheer up! You're the only one of us who has his very own cloud, and even better, it rains in bright orange! Don't you reckon that we could play some really fun games with a cloud like that?" Mark reluctantly agreed, because these days she was his only company, and didn't want her to leave as the others had.

Stephanie dared Mark to jump into the swimming pool, and then went and got the other kids while the water turned orange. All of the kids came and played in the pool, because the water being orange meant they could play hide and seek! Grudgingly, Mark had to admit that he had been having a lot of fun, but what he liked even more was playing the game "Wet the Cat".

Mark would find cats and run alongside them, causing them to get wet. With funny looks on their faces, they would run off at top speed and jump in the craziest ways. Before long, all the children gathered around Mark, and began thinking up new games they all could play together using the cloud.

For the first time ever, Mark started to see the positive side of things; even in those which at first had seemed so bad. Sophie, the prankster cloud; thought that she could now leave, because her work there had been done. Before floating away, Sophie gave Mark two days of multicolored rain, with which the children invented the most fun games ever.

Mark didn't complain when Sophie finally left, because now he knew to focus on the good in life. The best thing about Sophie's departure was that Mark was no longer soaking wet all day. Now he could go and do "dry" things with his new friends, and that's exactly what he did.

Secret # 7: The Power of Optimism

Defining the Power of Optimism:

Optimism is: a) having hopefulness and confidence, b) having a tendency to expect the best, and see the best, in all things.

Most researchers agree that optimism is largely a *learned* trait. That's wonderful news because if you aren't naturally an optimist, you can *learn* to be.

Optimistic parents are confident and speak positive words of encouragement to themselves and their children. Knowing their strengths and *working on* their weaknesses, lets parents position themselves and their children for ultimate success.

Form a vision (a mental picture) of yourself as a successful parent: bold and courageous, strong, effective, and successful. If you will hold that picture in your mind and continually dwell on what it takes to bring it to pass, you will begin to see astonishing changes.

As Napoleon Hill said, "What the mind of man can conceive, and believe, it can achieve."

Pessimism (continually dwelling on negative thoughts) is easy, but what are the results? Pessimists lose hope, feel a lack of control, expect failure, and resist change.

Both optimism and pessimism have consequences. If we get what we expect, we should expect what we want! By holding fast to positive expectations, you will be letting your incredible mind help you move toward your desired destiny.

In addition to your own destiny, how are you lighting the path for your child? Are you *expecting* them to be positive, happy, self-controlled, and self-disciplined?

Expectations are powerful. Set positive expectations and model optimistic behaviors, because the most powerful children on the planet are those who have *learned* to be optimistic.

Manifestation of Parents Lacking Optimism:

Parents lacking optimism are often:

* Negative and full of doom and gloom
* Use negative words
* Hold negative mental images in their minds

Pessimistic parents tend to hold on to images that result in corresponding negative outcomes—not only in their own lives, but also in the lives of their children.

Characteristics of an Optimistic Parent:
Optimistic parents:
- Have minds filled with positive thoughts of faith
- Are happy and joyful
- Visualize strength, confidence, and success.

Optimistic parents are fully aware that their minds will always try to complete anything they picture. Therefore, they work hard to continually formulate images of success. By practicing and modeling optimism, they consistently add value to their children.

Sayings of an Optimistic Parent:

"All things are possible."

"I believe all things work together for my good."

"I am strong, bold, and confident."

How to Build the Power of Optimism

Activities:

1. Practice forming vivid mental pictures of yourself and your children being happy, optimistic, and successful.

2. When obstacles appear in your life, try saying: "This is wonderful!" and then see how many reasons you can find why that may be true.

3. Rather than letting obstacles *expand* in your mind until they are enormous boulders, practice shrinking them until they become nothing more than helpful stepping-stones.

4. Take some time to reflect on all the positive results that come from a life filled with optimism:

   a. You will complain much less frequently
   b. You will look to the future with hope
   c. You will feel more in control
   d. You will embrace challenges because you expect success
   e. You will welcome new ideas
   f. You will embrace change

Those are fantastic results! *Learn* to be optimistic.

Parent Self-Esteem Survey # 7

Your child did the following:

( ) A. Played computer games
   past bedtime
( ) B. Forgot to wash the dishes
( ) C. Had fun in the park on a
   rainy day

Which action deserves the most attention from you? Please select an answer.

Answer

The correct answer is C. Enjoying life despite less than perfect circumstances is a great trait of an optimist. Always pay the most attention to the behavior you would like your child to repeat.

Parent Self Esteem Development Exercise

1. List at least two things you've learned in this chapter that will help you become more optimistic about your day, and your life.

2. List three reasons why you deserve to be optimistic about your future.

3. Think of something negative that happened recently. List three possible positive things that could result from that event.

4. How will being more optimistic improve your life?

5. How can you help your children and family members become more optimistic about their days?

Affirmations for Building the Power of Optimism

I choose to be optimistic.

I believe good things come to me.

I expect excellence from my day.

I am productive.

I believe in myself.

My optimistic attitude makes me happy.

I love being optimistic.

I unlock my potential through optimism.

I am confident.

I am courageous.

I am bold.

I am hopeful about my future.

I think about things that are true and lovely.

I am a strong leader.

Kids Growth Development Exercise

Growth happens through change. Help your children learn to view their circumstances with optimism. Children with healthy self-esteem welcome change and respond in positive ways.

(Assist your children with the completion of this activity)

A. List two positive results that could come from changing schools, getting a new teacher, or starting a new school year.

1. _____

2. _____

B. Are there any big changes happening now or coming soon in your family? List two ways you can help others in the family be happy in spite of those changes.

1. _____

2. _____

Draw a picture showcasing your ideas for responding to change in positive ways.

Power of Optimism Quotes

"Even if I knew that tomorrow the whole world would go to pieces, I would still plant my apple tree." **(Martin Luther)**

"Genius is one percent inspiration and ninety-nine percent perspiration." **(Thomas Edison)**

"The man who acquires the ability to take full possession of own mind may take possession of anything else to which he is justly entitled." **(Andrew Carnegie)**

"In the middle of difficulty lies opportunity." **(Albert Einstein)**

"Throw the shoulders back, let the heart sing, let the eyes flash, let the mind be lifted up, look upward and say to your self.... Nothing is impossible!" **(Norman Vincent Peale)**

"Don't judge each day by the harvest you reap, but by the seeds that you plant." **(Robert Louis Stevenson)**

"Act as if it was impossible to fail." ***(Dorothy Broude)***

"All who have accomplished great things have had a great aim, have fixed their gaze on a goal which was high, one which sometimes seemed impossible." **(Orison Swett Marden)**

"The essence of optimism is that it takes no account of the present, but it is a source of inspiration, of vitality and hope where others have resigned; it enables a man to hold his head high, to claim the future for himself and not abandon it to his enemy." **(Dietrich Bonhoeffer)**

Resources for Parents on the Subject of Optimism:

Suggested Books to Read for Younger Children:
-*Mama's Crows Gift* by Lory Britain
-*How Full is Your Bucket? For Kids* by Tom Rath

Suggested Books to Read for Older Children:
-*Promoting Positive Thinking* by Glynis Hannell
-*Mind Coach* by Daniel Amen

Suggested Books to Read for Parents:
-*Raising Resilient Children* by Robert Brooks
-*The Power of Attitude* by John C. Maxwell

Suggested Family Movies to Watch:
-*"America's Sweetheart Collection"* (1938)-Shirley Temple
-*"Happy Feet"* (2007)-Robin Williams

Parents can help build their child's self-esteem through encouragement, praise, and optimism.

What behaviors are you modeling for <u>your</u> children?

Secret # 8:
The Power of Gentleness

Story About Gentleness

There was once a little fish that was gentle, but very, lazy. Every day was a struggle because when it was time to get up, his parents had to shout at him again and again. And when there was some job he had to do, he would keep putting it off until there was hardly enough time left to do it. "What a lazy fish you are! You can't just keep leaving everything to the last minute." The other fish kept telling him.

"Bah! There's really no problem", scoffed the little fish, "I just take a bit longer to get around to doing things, that's all."

The fish spent all summer swimming and playing. When autumn came, they began to prepare for the long journey to a warmer section of the ocean. But the little fish, lazy as ever, kept putting it off. He felt quite sure that there would be plenty of time to prepare, until one day, when he woke up and all the other fish were gone.

Just like every other day, several of his friends had tried to wake him. Half asleep, he told them he would get up later, and went right back to sleep. That day was the day of the great journey and everyone knew the rule: You had to be ready to leave because there were thousands of fish, and they weren't going to wait around for anyone. As the little fish didn't know how to make the journey alone, he realized that his laziness had caused him to spend the long, cold winter on his own.

At the beginning, he spent a lot of time crying, but he had to admit that it was his own fault, and he needed to be gentle with himself. He knew that when he put his mind to it, he could do things well. Making the decision to be gentle with himself, he put his laziness aside, and began to prepare for the winter.

First, he spent days looking for a place that was best protected from the cold. He found one between some rocks, and there he made a new home. It was well built with branches, stones, and shells. He then worked tirelessly to fill his new home with sea grass and algae, enough to last the whole winter. Finally, he dug a little pool into a rock, so he would have enough water. With his new home perfectly prepared, he trained himself to be able to endure the worst ocean storms, by getting by on very little food and water.

Although many would not have believed it, all these preparations helped the gentle fish to survive through the winter. Of course, he suffered greatly, and not a day went by without him regretting having been such a "lazy" little fish. When spring finally arrived, his old friends returned, and were all filled with joy and surprise, that the little fish was still alive. They could hardly believe that such a "lazy" fish had managed to build such a wonderful home. The fish agreed that he had turned into the most hardworking fish of the school, and that he should be put in charge of organizing the great journey next year.

When that time came, the fish were so well prepared, and they had time left over to invent an early morning wake-up song. From that day forward, (regardless of how lazy it was), would ever have to spend the winter alone again.

Secret # 8: The Power of Gentleness

Defining the Power of Gentleness:

Gentleness is a character trait marked by: calmness, tenderness, kindness, and a pleasant, good-natured personality. A gentle person is also generally known for being compassionate, considerate, and warm-hearted.

Parents who have mastered the art of gentleness have learned to manage their thoughts and emotions skillfully. This sounds easy, but it's not. Try being gentle and remaining calm when someone is "in your face" and being difficult…gentleness isn't our "normal" response!

The easy or normal response is to treat people the way they treat us. When we respond instead with care or kindness, we are demonstrating the power of gentleness.

Remember, we may not know what could be causing another person to talk or act in a certain way. It isn't always obvious externally when someone is hurting inside. The gentle person looks past rough exteriors, and responds to the hidden hurt or insecurities of another, with care and forgiveness.

Gentleness is demonstrated not only in our actions, but also in our thoughts, words, and intentions. Our families and friends offer us many opportunities to demonstrate gentleness. Nurture others through your actions and give of your best: a gentle touch, some caring words, a listening ear, and a compassionate heart.

Help your children master gentleness by being a successful role model. When your children are able to feel good being around you, it's an indication that your gentleness has touched their hearts. Children love the warm-heartedness and tenderness of gentle parents.

Manifestation of Parents Lacking Gentleness

Parents lacking gentleness often:

- Communicate with their children by screaming and shouting
- Are chronically in a rush or hurry
- Are selfish, full of pride, arrogant, violence, and insecure

Characteristics of Gentle Parents

Gentle parents are usually:

- Calm, patient, humble, and attentive listeners
- Responsibility for their own happiness
- Care for others
- Care for the planet.

Outwardly, it would appear that gentle parents always put others first. In general that is true, but there is a deeper principle at work: these parents have *first* invested time in developing themselves for greater good.

We can only give from what we have. If we have character deficiencies we haven't addressed, we can only sow from deficiency. Poor seed equals poor crops.

Learn to pay attention to your own needs, desires, and deficiencies. Attend to them with discipline, and then give from your strengths with joy...the joy that comes from gentleness.

Sayings of a Gentle Parent:

"What is making you feel weary and burdened?"

"I forgive you."

"What ideas do you have?"

How to Build the Power of Gentleness

Activities:

1. Review your personal mission statement and life goals every day.
2. Keep your highest aspirations forefront in your mind. This will allow you to live from a place of peace, purpose, and gentleness.
3. Make a list of ways you could be gentle with yourself.
4. _ACT_ on at least one of these ideas every day. Here are some samples:
    a. Collect some hugs. Research has shown that we need at least 8 hugs per day to survive, and 10 or more to thrive!
    b. Relax. Turn on some calming music, light a candle, and take a bath.
    c. Turn off the television
    d. Turn off the computer
    e. Spend some time outdoors in nature instead.
5. Make a list of ways you could demonstrate gentleness with your children, family, and community.
6. Use the ideas from your list, to connect with five family members and five friends, within the next 30 days.

Parent Self-Esteem Survey # 8

Your child does the following:

( ) A. Wakes up late for school

( ) B. Hits his/her sibling

( ) C. Completes one page of
reading

Which action deserves the most attention from you? Please select an answer.

Answer

The correct answer is **C**. Always pay the most attention to
the behavior you would like your child to practice.

Parent Self Esteem Development Exercise

1. List three "out of the box" ideas for being gentle with yourself. (You are a unique individual… How can you treat yourself in some unique ways? What would be special just for you?)

2. List two personal character defects you will deliberately work to correct in order to increase your gentleness with your children.

3. If someone asked you for advice on how to improve their level of calmness, what answer would you give them? How can you apply that same advice to your own life?

4. Who do you know that demonstrates the power of gentleness? Arrange to have tea or a meal with one or more of those people, and ask them for advice.

Affirmations for Building the
Power of Gentleness

I choose to be gentle.

I enjoy being gentle.

I speak gently to myself.

I look for ways to be gentle with others.

I am gentle with my parenting style.

Gentleness is part of my character.

I remain calm during stressful moments.

I control my emotions.

I am humble.

I love being gentle.

I respect my children.

My children are gentle with me.

I respond gently to the instructions of others.

Kids' Gentleness Exercise

Skill development is foundational for all children.
As you work with your child to develop gentleness, remember
that you are their most important role model.
Be considerate. Show compassion and forgiveness.

(Help your children with completing this assignment.)

1. What does it mean to be gentle? List your ideas.

   _____

2. What can you do today to show gentleness to one of your family members? List your ideas, decide which one is your favorite, and go do it right now!

   _____

Draw a picture showcasing your ideas for being gentle with others

Gentleness Quotes

"I choose gentleness…Nothing is won by force. I choose to be gentle. If I raise my voice may it only be in praise. If I clench my fist, may it only be in prayer. If I make a demand, may it be only of myself." **(Max Lucado)**

"A wise mother knows: It is her state of consciousness that matters. Her gentleness and clarity command respect. Her love creates security." **(Vimala McClure)**

"The process of breaking down fear was always my greatest challenge and it was made easier by the careful work and the gentle voices of my female workers." **(Muhammad Yunus)**

"The way to overcome the angry man is with gentleness, the evil man with goodness, the miser with generosity, and the liar with truth." **(Indian Proverb)**

"Gentleness is the antidote for cruelty." **(Phaedrus)**

"I have three precious things which I hold fast and prize. The first is gentleness; the second is frugality; the third is humility, which keeps me from putting myself before others. Be gentle and you can be bold; be frugal and you can be liberal; avoid putting yourself before others and you can become a leader among men." **Lao Tzu**

"I learned it is the weak who are cruel, and that gentleness is to be expected only from the strong." **Leo Rosten**

Resources for Parents on the
Subject of Gentleness:

Suggested Books to Read for Younger Children:
-<u>Hi, I am Straw Beary</u> by Melody Calrson
-<u>What Your First Grader Needs to Know</u> by E. D. Hirsch
Jr.

Suggested Books to Read for Older Children:
-<u>Honey for a Child's Heart</u> by Gladys Hunt
-<u>The Book of Virtues for Young People</u> by Catherine
Ryan Hyde

Suggested Books to Read for Parents:
-<u>Books that Builds Character</u> by William Kilpatrick

Suggested Family Movies to Watch:
-"Gentle Giant" (1997)-Dennis Weaver
-"Gentle Ben" (2003)-Dean Caine

Non-Verbal communication may be more important in building a child's healthy self-esteem than verbal communication.

"What you DO speaks louder than what you say."

Are your actions modeling behaviors you want your child to emulate?

Secret # 9:
The Power of Self Control

Story About Self-Control

Once upon a time, there was a little glutton who would only ever eat chips and chocolate. One day, while out shopping with his mother, he found an old magnifying glass. He liked it so much, that his mother bought it for him, and as soon as he could, he used it to look at a little ant. It was great! The ant looked so big, but then a strange thing happened. When he took the magnifying glass away, the ant stayed the same size it had appeared through the glass.

Very surprised, the boy kept working toward new discoveries, and he found that anything he looked at through the magnifying glass would get bigger, and stayed that way.

Suddenly, he realized how he could best use this secret of his, and ran home. When he got there, he took all the chips and chocolates, and made them gigantic with his magnifying glass. Then, he completely stuffed himself until he could eat nothing more. The next morning he woke up totally swollen, a bit yellow, and with a horrible stomach ache. When the doctor came to see him, he said, "This is the worst case of an upset stomach he had ever seen." Night and day, the little glutton suffered so much that for a long time he didn't want to hear any mention of large amounts of food.

His parents were very happy about this. Thanks to their son's latest gluttony, they now had a pantry full of the foods he could eat to be healthy.

What's more, he gave up being a glutton who only ever ate chips and chocolate. He wanted nothing to do with them.

And so it was, the little glutton learned if you have too many of the best things in life, you will not be able to enjoy them without using self-control. He decided to keep the magnifying glass in a box, until he found something that would really be worth making bigger.

How about you? What would you use the magnifying glass for?

Secret # 9: The Power of Self Control

Defining the Power of Self-Control:

Self-control is the ability to control your emotions, behavior, and desires. It involves self-management, and in that sense, means having command or mastery over your own behavior. The development of self-control is a crucial step in the process of building healthy self-esteem.

Controlling your thoughts is an excellent area in which to begin the practice of self-control. Thoughts multiplied over time become attitudes, and attitudes then influence our behavior. Negative thoughts lead to negative behaviors and positive thoughts lead to positive behaviors. Positive behaviors produce success.

Behavior is an external mirror to the inner thoughts we permit. Negative behaviors have direct correlations to negative thoughts. Positive thoughts will lead to the behaviors we desire.

If we are successfully able to identify the thoughts that produce negative behaviors, we are then able to *change* those thoughts as they occur. Monitoring our thoughts is a daily assignment, and we need to be ever vigilant.

Another useful practice in mastering self-control is to become conscious of the words that come out of our mouths. Our words are powerful! They have the ability to build up or to destroy others.

Positive words work for the good of our selves and others. If you've been practicing the affirmations in this book, you'll know with a certainty the truth of that statement. Positive and encouraging words not only build you up personally, they build up your family members, *and* they help build your child's self-esteem.

137

Your children cannot monitor your thoughts. They can only monitor your words and your behaviors. Self-control is your responsibility. Please take this responsibility seriously. Your words and your behaviors are major influences on what happens in your family.

Manifestation of Parents Lacking Self-Control
Parents lacking self-control:
- Abuse themselves and/or their children
- Are careless (or even clueless), about their life mission, purpose, and influence on others
- Often let negativity and criticism become the standard forms of communication in the home

Characteristics of Self-Controlled Parents
Self-controlled parents:
- Monitor their thoughts
- Speak only what they want to be true
- Reject all negative emotions
- Refuse to harbor thoughts that produce sadness, anger, or negativity

Sayings of a Parent with Self-Control:
"I am in control of my behavior."

"I am in control of my emotions."

"I am in control of my thoughts."

"I allow only positive thoughts about myself and others."

How to Build the Power of Self-Control

Activities:

1. Take a look at the behaviors that get you into trouble. Write down the thoughts that produce those behaviors.

2. Rewrite a positive thought for each negative behavior, and repeat the new thoughts daily until you experience positive results with yourself and others.

3. Practice delayed gratification. Foregoing immediate satisfaction is part of learning self-control. Good things come to those who wait, not to those who put everything on their credit cards!

4. Insert a pause between your thoughts, and your vocal chords or actions. Our immediate gut reactions usually get us into trouble. No one will notice the extra second or two you take, to be sure you are giving a considered reaction.

5. Practice "keeping it clean" (your mouth, that is). Anger and foul language are signs that you are lacking self-control. When you are irritated or distressed, take time to *think*, before you speak or act.

Parent Self-Esteem Survey # 9

Your child does the following:

( ) A. Refuses to eat dinner

( ) B. Takes out the garbage

( ) C. Slams the door

Which action deserves the most attention from you? Please select an answer.

Answer

The correct answer is **B**. Always pay the most attention to the behavior you would like your child to practice.

Parent Self Esteem Development Exercise

1. Mentally rate your level of self-control on a scale of 1-10. What steps can you take to move higher on the scale?

2. Self-control takes effort and practice. List three daily irritations that will give you opportunities to practice. Decide in advance how you will respond to those irritations in the future.

3. Why is self-control important? How can your personal practice of self-control add value to your life, and to the lives of your children?

4. Who do you know who has powerful self-control? Arrange to spend time with them, and ask them to share their wisdom on this topic. Discuss your new knowledge with your children.

Affirmations for Building the Power of Self-Control

I choose to practice self-control.

I manage my emotions.

I take control of my thoughts.

I think about things that are true and authentic.

My thoughts about others are loving and peaceful.

I carefully monitor my words.

I speak only words of empowerment.

I speak kind words to myself.

Self-control is an easy habit for me to practice.

I take responsibility for my actions.

I set goals for managing my priorities.

I manage my time wisely.

I choose to prepare my day ahead of time.

I keep my focus and limit distractions.

Kids' Self-Control Development Exercise

Self-control is difficult even for adults, especially if we never had an adult model it well for us when we were kids. Take time to discuss self-control issues with your children. Do your best to model appropriate responses for them to learn from.

(Assist your children with the completion of this exercise)

1. Did anything make you upset or angry today?

   _____

2. What did you do when that happened? (How did you feel? What did you say?)

   _____

3. What would have happened if you had walked away for a few minutes to cool off, instead of having an outburst?

   _____

Draw a picture showing angry people on one side and happy people on the other side. Discuss what makes the differences between each group.

Self-control Quotes

"The best day of your life is the one on which you decide your life is your own. No apologies or excuses. No one to lean one, rely on, or blame. The gift is yours-it is an amazing journey-and you alone are responsible for the quality of it. This is the day your life really begins." **(Bob Moawad)**

"Everyone must choose between two pains: The pain of discipline or the pain of regret." **(Jim Rhon)**

"You must admit you have self-control before you can use it." **(Carrie Latet)**

"First we make our habits, then, our habits make us." **(Charles C. Noble)**

"The happiness of a man in this life does not consist in the absence of but the mastery of his passions." **(Alfred Lord Tennyson)**

"My fault, my failure is not in the passions I have, but in my lack of control of them." **(Jack Kerouac)**

"What we do upon some great occasion will probably depend on what we already are; and what we are will be the results of previous years of self-discipline." **(H.P. Liddon)**

"If you do not conquer self, you will be conquered by self." **(Napoleon Hill)**

Resources for Parents on the Subject of Self-Control:

Suggested Books to Read for Younger Children:
-<u>It's Hard to Be Five</u> by Jamie Lee Curtis
-<u>Big Words for Little People</u> by Jamie Lee Curtis

Suggested Books to Read for Older Children:
-<u>The Feelings Book</u> by Dr. Lynda Madison
-<u>Stick up for Yourself</u> by Greshen Kaufman

Suggested Books to Read for Parents:
-<u>The Secrets of Self-Control</u> by Richard Ganz

Suggested Family Movies to Watch:
-"Medea's Big Happy Family" (2011)-Tyler Perry
-"Swiss Family Robinson" (2002)-John Mills

Bonus Secret:

The Power of
Real Connection

The Power of Real Connection

Email, Twitter, Facebook, LinkedIn, MySpace, YouTube, Digg, Blogs, and a legion of others, are the current leaders of the new and innovative ways parents can now **<u>disconnect</u>** with their children 24/7.

Digital photos, computers, books and music have all contributed to a new generation of "digital children." Unfortunately, they are being digitized and prepped for "digital fluency" not relationships. The power of real connection has nothing to do with digitization. Real connection is investing a large amount of quality time daily with your children, with a limited use of electronic toys.

Substituting a physical relationship for an electronic one with your children is a character trait that belongs to low self-esteem parents. Those who are not prepared to connect strategically with their children, or are proactively using a limited amount of this technology, will suffer the most.

Children of this generation are more likely to own a cell phone, than a book about values or the power of self-responsibility. Using "Touchnology" and "Magnetic Sensors" are just some of the tools skillfully being used by most children, to communicate with friends about the latest styles, games, and social news without parent interference or censorship.

With a 900 channel TV, (a babysitting gadget), and unlimited, downloadable webpages, many children do not stand a chance against this lethal attack for access to their mind.

Apple has sold almost 60 million IPhones worldwide, while Google's Android OS is growing at 886% per year, and is now activating over 160,000 devices a day. This is clearly not a plan to improve real connection.

Even though, parents are becoming more aware of the disconnect and isolation they have from their children, most are at a disadvantage, because they refuse the knowledge, understanding and wisdom, of how embracing this technology could improve and save the relationship with their children.

A parenting shift must take place immediately, before it's too late. Mobile phones with a connection to social networking are no longer for adults. Most children as early as seven years old, are fully engaged using social network at a whole new level. Today, children attending middle and high schools have access to chat rooms, and porn introduction is now easily available through advertisements that connect with your child's mind at a faster pace.

Some tips for using technology to improve the relationship with your child include:

- *Using multimedia computers to increase your child's reading potential*
- *Using the internet to create and build an educational database for each grade level*
- *Using cell phones for texting empowerment quotes at the beginning and end of your child's day*

The most powerful and effective marketing gurus use targeted campaign ads to capitalize on the vulnerability of children for reaching (the prey), who are isolated and left alone without a family purpose, vision, or mission.

This is a wake up call for parents refusing to create a stable home environment that motivates and inspires their children with and without this digitized age. Parenting children is now at a crisis stage due to technology ignorance practiced by many parents.

According to the Campaign for a Commercial Free Childhood:
- Teen girls who watch more than 14 hours of rap videos, are more likely to have multiple sex partners and be diagnosed with a STD.
- On the top 10 CDs in 1999, 42% of the songs contained sexual content, 19% including direct descriptions of sexual intercourse.
- On average, music videos contained 93 sexual situations (including eleven "hard core" scenes), depicting behaviors such as intercourse and oral sex.

Parents must get involved and become educated in how media and technology affect their children's growth and development. There is a dark side to this technology, and being ignorant to its devices is not the proper response for helping your children.

What do you understand about internet safety? How can you help your children avoid cyber bullying? Are your children addicted to texting? What tactics are you using to protect your children from self-destruction? How can you tell if your computers or phones are being hacked?

Internet predators are waiting to capitalize on this level of ignorance. According to statistics, teens are exposed to over 49 hours of media consumption per week, for entertainment purposes only. This does not count media consumption during school time. This high level of exposure and enslavement to media stimulation is unhealthy and strategically designed to steal your children's mind.

My advice to parents is to become proactive now. By the time you are done reading this chapter, your child could be one of many that use this technology as a gateway "drug" to provide a state of ecstasy that chemically alter their brain, leaving them desperate for more digital stimulation.

I challenge all parents to *immediately* set a higher standard for their families, by refusing to be a victim to this digital age. Remember this: the only lasting, effective solution that children crave is a true connection of "live" experiences with their parents, using both the "real" and "virtual" worlds.

Scriptural Secrets for
Building Self-Esteem

Scriptural Secret # 1: The Power of Love

[Let your] love be sincere (a real thing); hate what
is evil [loathe all ungodliness, turn in horror from
wickedness], but hold fast to that which is good.
Romans 12: 9 (AMP)

Scriptural Secret # 2: The Power of Joy

Be happy [in your faith] and rejoice and be
glad-hearted continually (always).
1 Thessalonians 5: 16 (AMP)

Scriptural Secret # 3: The Power of Peace

You will guard him and keep him in perfect and constant
peace whose mind [both its inclination and its character]
is stayed on You, because he commits himself to You,
leans on You, and hopes confidently in You.
Isaiah 26: 3 (AMP)

Scriptural Secret # 4: The Power of Patience

Be assured and understand that the trial and proving of your
faith bring out endurance and steadfastness and patience.
James 1: 3 (AMP)

Scriptural Secret # 5: The Power of Kindness

He who is kind to the poor lends to the Lord, and
he will reward him for what he has done.
Proverbs 19:17 (AMP)

Scriptural Secret # 6: The Power of Goodness

What shall I return to the Lord for all his goodness to me?
Psalm 116:12 (AMP)

Scriptural Secret # 7: The Power of Optimism

He who is faithful in a very little [thing] is faithful also
in much, and he who is dishonest and unjust in a very
little [thing] is dishonest and unjust also in much.
Luke 16: 10 (AMP)

Scriptural Secret # 8: The Power of Gentleness

A gentle answer turns away wrath, but
a harsh word stirs up anger.
Proverbs 15:1 (AMP)

Scriptural Secret # 9: The Power of Self Control

Like a city whose walls are broken down
so is a man who lacks self-control.
Proverbs 25:28 (AMP)

Appendix A

Bonus Affirmations for Building Healthy Self-Esteem

Bonus Affirmations for Building Healthy Self-Esteem

I am confident.

I am focused.

I follow a vision plan.

I set priorities.

I understand my daily mission.

I am self-disciplined.

I am responsible for my thoughts.

I speak only words of empowerment.

I understand my purpose in life.

I am full of potential.

I am forgiving.

I value my time.

I am strong and healthy.

I am victorious!

Appendix B

Bonus Parent/Child Activities for Building Healthy Self-Esteem

Bonus Parent/Child Activities for Building Healthy Self-Esteem

Here are four additional activities you can try:

Parent/Child Activity # 1: Help your child create a personal vision board of their goals for the next 3 months. Add powerful, stimulating, and encouraging pictures for each goal. Display the vision board in your child's bedroom. Celebrate your child's accomplishment with praise!

Parent/Child Activity #2: Help your child identify and write down a list of negative thoughts they have a hard time controlling. Now spend some time helping your child come up with ways to manage those negative thoughts. Implement at least one idea within the next twenty-four hours.

Parent/Child Activity #3: Help your child learn to add value to the community. Ask questions such as, "What can you do today to brighten your teacher's day?" or "How can you help to improve our community today?"

Parent/Child Activity #4: Help your (older) children learn to set priorities. Setting priorities is connected to mastering self-discipline. See what interesting answers arise when you ask your child to:
1. Write down two important things they would like to complete within the next 24 hours.
2. Write down four important things they would like to accomplish within the next 30 days.

Have FUN with the activities…the interactions you have with your children are *priceless (!)* and can have tremendous impact on their level of self-esteem. They say you can't have your cake and eat it too…these activities may be the exceptions to the rule. Enjoy!

Download Your Parental Toolkit Today!

THE 10 MOST POWERFUL PARENTING SKILLS ON THE PLANET

www.BrooksandBrooksFoundation.org

Made in the USA
San Bernardino, CA
21 December 2015